A Christian Man's Guide to Love and Marriage in the 21st Century

(Why Everything You Think You Know Is Wrong)

Don Riefstahl

A Christian Man's Guide to Love and Marriage in the 21st Century
Copyright © 2013 Don Riefstahl

Cover design by Don Riefstahl
Stock photos licensed from www.colourbox.com

Unless otherwise identified, Scripture quotations are from the HOLY BIBLE, NEW INTERNATIONAL VERSION©. Copyright © 1973, 1978, 1984 by International Bible Society. Used by permission of Zondervan Publishing House. All rights reserved.

This book is published under a Creative Commons license.
You are free, and encouraged:

To Share – to copy, distribute and transmit this work
To Remix – to adapt the work

Under the following conditions:

Noncommercial – You may not use this work for commercial purposes without express permission from the copyright holder.

Attribution – You must attribute the work in the manner specified by the author.

Other Rights – In no way are any of the following affected by this license:

- Your fair dealing or fair use rights, or other applicable copyright exceptions and limitations;
- Rights other persons may have in either the work itself or in how the work is used such as publicity or privacy rights.

For more information, contact donald.riefstahl@yahoo.com

First Edition v1.01 / Updated September 15th, 2013

For Ginger, who has been such an encouragement as I struggle on my journey from nice guy to good man.

Contents

	Introduction..	7
1	*The Red Pill*..	9
2	*Is the Bible Relevant?*...	13
3	*The Biblical Order*...	15
4	*Complementary Natures*...	25
5	*The Rebellion Against God's Order*..........................	29
6	*A World Without Bicycles*.......................................	35
7	*On Civilization, Feminism and "Manning Up"*..........	41
8	*Rediscovering Masculinity*......................................	53
9	*Alpha Beta Soup*..	57
10	*Shaken, Not Stirred*..	63
11	*Red Pill Dating*..	67
12	*The Sexual Marketplace*..	73
13	*The Institution Formerly Known as Marriage*............	79
14	*How to Choose a Good Wife*....................................	85
15	*Conclusion*...	91
	Resources...	95

Introduction

Let me begin by saying that I am not a writer. I have never written a book before, nor have I ever had any desire to do so. To be perfectly honest, I didn't even want to write this one. I am a happily married computer technician living a simple, comfortable life and I would really prefer not to rock the boat.

I expect that the message in this book will be poorly received by many people, and that they will be very angry with me for sharing it. Nevertheless, because I believe it is desperately needed, I am willing to risk my own comfort and reputation to share it with you.

In the following pages I will be exploring several topics which, when taken together, will give the reader an overview of the landscape facing young men in America today. In addition, I will offer some practical advice for successfully navigating the uncertain terrain of today's dating landscape.

This book is short by design in an effort to make it easily accessible to even the most casual of readers; therefore it was necessary at times to paint with a very broad brush. While I would concede that there is room for debate about many of the points that are made and topics discussed, I nevertheless believe that I have provided an accurate sketch of the issues at hand.

I would also like to point out that this book relies heavily on the work of others. I have included lengthy quotes from many sources, both Christian and non-Christian, and most of the ideas presented did not originate with me.

There is a lot of good information out there, but because it's scattered so broadly it's sometimes difficult to see the forest for the trees. This book is simply my attempt to provide the reader with a brief overview of the big picture.

Finally, I realize that not everyone will agree with everything I say. If you find yourself in disagreement with something I've written, I make the following recommendation: eat the meat and spit out the bones.

I've found that, by approaching the world in this way, it's possible to learn something valuable almost every day and from nearly any source. Don't let a few minor quibbles distract you from the overall message.

It is my sincere hope that the information contained in this book will challenge your perception of the world around you and provide you with some new tools for the journey ahead.

Grace and peace to you,

Don

Chapter One
The Red Pill

If you are anything like me (and if you are a young Christian man who was raised in today's culture then I suspect that you are), you've had more than a little trouble in your dating life. You've done everything exactly the way you were taught, but for some reason women just don't see you as anything more than a friend.

You've worked hard at not being like those "other guys". You've made yourself emotionally vulnerable. You've gone out of your way to make sure women feel comfortable around you by building solid friendships with them, hoping that someday one of them would see that you are a worthy man and choose to settle down with you.

But, to your surprise, you've watched them date jerk after jerk, all the while telling you that you are "such a great guy" who is "going to make some lucky girl really happy someday."

Sound familiar? Yeah, I told you we were a lot alike. And here's the sad part – it's not just the two of us. It's not even just a few of us. There's a whole generation of young men out there who are building their entire mating strategy around the idea that young women are desperately trying to find a nice guy. The expectation is that, once a woman finds a nice guy, she will fall in love with him and they will live happily ever after.

I hate to be the one to tell you this, but it's not that simple. Not even close. There's a reason women tend to date jerks instead of nice guys, and it has nothing to do with them not realizing just how nice those nice guys really are.

There is a worldview in which the answer to this mystery is finally revealed; those of us who have stumbled onto it call it "The Red Pill". The name is taken from the movie *The Matrix*, in which Neo is offered a choice between two pills – a red one and a blue one.

If he takes the red pill, he will finally see the world as it really is. If he takes the blue pill, he will return to his old life and never even remember being offered the choice. The catch, of course, is that if he takes the red pill, he can never go back. Once you know how a magician does his tricks you will never look at his show the same way again.

It's up to you to decide whether you want to take the red pill or the blue pill. I'll tell you right up front that the red pill can be very bitter at first, and it does take a little bit of the magic out of romance. But the discomfort is only temporary.

It's a bit like finding out that there isn't really a Santa Claus. Sure, there's an initial shock, but as you adjust to the real world you'll find that seeing things as they truly are has its upside.

The red pill, though bitter, will provide you with the tools necessary to have a successful marriage. That's no small thing these days. You've seen the statistics – half of all marriages now end in divorce. How many couples from the remaining half do you suppose are living lives of marital bliss?

I don't know the percentage, but based on observation I suspect it's a pretty low number. Personally, if there's something out there that can increase my chances of having a happy, successful marriage then I want to know about it. But that's just me. You'll have to make your own decision.

Just keep in mind that, like Morpheus in *The Matrix*, all I offer is the truth – nothing more.

Chapter Two
Is the Bible Relevant?

So, you're a Christian. That means you are living your life with a 4,000-year-old book as your guide. Some people would (and do) call that crazy. They say the Bible was written for a different people in a different time. They say it's been translated so many times that nobody knows for sure what it really even says. They say the entire thing is open to individual interpretation and so it means something different to everybody.

Those are fair charges; however, they are outside the scope of this book. I am not writing an in-depth work of apologetics; I am writing a dating guide. As a young Christian man you can and should seek the answers to these questions. I already have, and I've come to the conclusion that the Bible is a reliable, accurate book that is meant to be taken literally in most cases.

But even if the Bible is reliable, is it really relevant in your search for a wife? What could it possibly have to say that relates to the world of dating in the 21st century?

Quite a lot, it turns out. As our Creator, God knows a thing or two about men and women. He knows what works and what doesn't. And He's given us some pretty clear instructions, if only we would take them seriously.

I will, therefore, be approaching Scripture with the assumption that it says what it means and means what it says. That may sound obvious, but you'd be surprised how many people will try to wiggle out of certain passages or simply ignore them altogether.

We live in a time in which the highest good is to never offend anyone for any reason. The Scriptural ideas highlighted in this book will offend some people – possibly you. I only ask that you judge the message on its own merits. Don't focus on whether or not it's offensive to modern sensibilities. Instead, ask yourself if it could be *true*.

Chapter Three
The Biblical Order

Our journey begins as all journeys do: at the beginning. The creation story in Genesis sets the stage for everything that is to follow. It's a familiar story, and if you grew up in the church you've probably heard it a million times. In fact, you've probably heard it so many times that your eyes glaze over whenever somebody brings it up:

> *The serpent tempted Eve, Eve ate the fruit, Adam ate the fruit, yada yada yada – curse on mankind.*

Yeah, that's the gist of it. But if you look closer, there are actually some huge implications in this story that have somehow gone largely unnoticed. Why don't you read it with a fresh set of eyes and see if you catch anything you've never noticed before:

> *Then the Lord God formed a man from the dust of the ground and breathed into his nostrils the breath of life, and the man became a living being*
>
> ...

> *The Lord God took the man and put him in the Garden of Eden to work it and take care of it. And the Lord God commanded the man, "You are free to eat from any tree in the garden; but you must not eat from the tree of the knowledge of good and evil, for when you eat from it you will certainly die."*
>
> ...
>
> *But for Adam no suitable helper was found. So the Lord God caused the man to fall into a deep sleep; and while he was sleeping, he took one of the man's ribs and then closed up the place with flesh. Then the Lord God made a woman from the rib he had taken out of the man, and he brought her to the man. The man said,*
>
> *"This is now bone of my bones*
> *and flesh of my flesh;*
> *she shall be called 'woman,'*
> *for she was taken out of man."*
> *- Genesis 2:7-23 (NIV)*

Did you see it? No? What we have here, right at the beginning of the Bible, is the origin of the Biblical Order. This hierarchy is present throughout the rest of the Bible and can be thought of as a chain of command:

God > Man > Woman

> *Now I want you to realize that the head of every man is Christ, and the head of the woman is man, and the head of Christ is God.*
> *- 1 Corinthians 11:3 (NIV)*

A man is subject to the authority of God, while his wife is subject to the authority of both God and her husband. This pecking order may seem objectionable to our modern society, but throughout the rest of this book I will attempt to show you how this is not only the correct way for a Christian to approach marriage, but also the only approach to marriage that will make most couples genuinely happy together. It is, in a word, natural – even if it doesn't seem so at first blush.

So, now that we know *what* the Biblical Order is, let's see if we can determine *why* it is.

First of all, we have Adam created by God directly from the dust of the ground while Eve was created from a part of Adam. This means that woman is quite literally a variation of man. This isn't to say that women are inferior to men, only that their role is supplemental. Woman was created to be man's helpmeet:

> *The Lord God said, "It is not good for the man to be alone. I will make a helper suitable for him."*
> *- Genesis 2:18 (NIV)*
>
> *For man did not come from woman, but woman from man; neither was man created for woman, but woman for man.*
> *- 1 Corinthians 11:7-9 (NIV)*

The other piece of the puzzle is found in the fall and subsequent curse of mankind. Let's pick the story back up in Genesis 3:

> *Now the serpent was more crafty than any of the wild animals the Lord God had made. He said to the woman, "Did God really say, 'You must not eat from any tree in the garden'?"*
>
> *The woman said to the serpent, "We may eat fruit from the trees in the garden, but God did say, 'You must not eat fruit from the tree that is in the middle of the garden, and you must not touch it, or you will die.'"*
>
> *"You will not certainly die," the serpent said to the woman. "For God knows that when you eat from it your eyes will be opened, and you will be like God, knowing good and evil."*

When the woman saw that the fruit of the tree was good for food and pleasing to the eye, and also desirable for gaining wisdom, she took some and ate it. She also gave some to her husband, who was with her, and he ate it. Then the eyes of both of them were opened, and they realized they were naked; so they sewed fig leaves together and made coverings for themselves.

Then the man and his wife heard the sound of the Lord God as he was walking in the garden in the cool of the day, and they hid from the Lord God among the trees of the garden. But the Lord God called to the man, "Where are you?"

He answered, "I heard you in the garden, and I was afraid because I was naked; so I hid."

And he said, "Who told you that you were naked? Have you eaten from the tree that I commanded you not to eat from?"

The man said, "The woman you put here with me—she gave me some fruit from the tree, and I ate it."
- Genesis 3:1-12 (NIV)

What we see here is two people committing two different sins. While Adam and Eve both sinned by eating the fruit, they actually sinned in completely different ways because they each had a different motivation for doing so.

If you're at all familiar with the rest of the story, you'll notice that Satan didn't flat-out lie to Eve (her eyes were indeed opened to good and evil); he merely deceived her. Eve's sin was placing relative truth above absolute truth:

Absolute Truth:
"You may surely eat of every tree of the garden, but of the tree of the knowledge of good and evil you shall not eat, for in the day that you eat of it you shall surely die."
- Genesis 2:16-17 (NIV)

> **Relative Truth:**
> *So when the woman saw that the tree was good for food, and that it was a delight to the eyes, and that the tree was to be desired to make one wise, she took of its fruit and ate.*
> *- Genesis 3:6 (NIV)*

Adam, on the other hand, was not deceived. Rather, he sinned by intentionally ignoring God's command and going along with his wife even though he knew better:

> *"Because you have listened to the voice of your wife*
> *and have eaten of the tree*
> *of which I commanded you,*
> *'You shall not eat of it,'*
> *cursed is the ground because of you;*
> *in pain you shall eat of it all the days of your life."*
> *- Genesis 3:17 (NIV)*

Part of Eve's punishment for placing relative truth above absolute truth was that she would now be under the authority of her husband, who was not deceived:

> *"Your desire shall be for your husband,*
> *and he shall rule over you."*
> *- Genesis 3:16 (NIV)*

These two things together then – the secondary creation of Eve and her curse for placing relative truth above absolute truth – are the foundation for the Biblical Order:

> *I do not permit a woman to teach or to exercise authority over a man … For Adam was formed first, then Eve; and Adam was not deceived, but the woman was deceived and became a transgressor.*
> *- 1 Timothy 2:12-14 (NIV)*

So, we see that women are essentially assigned a sidekick role while men get to play the superhero. After learning this, many of my male readers are undoubtedly doing a victory dance while my female readers are likely sharpening their pitch forks and lighting their torches.

Well, please hold your horses for just a few more minutes because we've still a lot of ground to cover.

Guys, I hate to rain on your victory dance, but there's a lot more to being at the top of the proverbial food chain than strutting around in a cape and bossing your trusty sidekick around:

> *With great power comes great responsibility.*

Yeah, I know, that's not the Bible – that's *Spiderman*. But it's definitely a biblical concept:

> *From everyone who has been given much, much will be demanded.*
> *- Luke 12:48 (NIV)*

Basically, as the leader of your relationship, the buck stops with you. If there's a problem that needs to be addressed, you're the one God is going to hold responsible. Marriage author Athol Kay likens the relationship between a husband and a wife to that of a Captain and First Officer:

> *I've come to understand it as being a Captain and First Officer relationship. And yes I first thought of this as a Star Trek metaphor (I don't dress up for conventions understand, I just like the shows) though it's basically standard for commercial airliners and military chain of command. As Wikipedia describes a First Officer…*
>
>> *"In commercial aviation, the first officer is the second pilot (sometimes referred to as the "co-pilot") of an aircraft. The first officer is second-in-command of the aircraft, to the captain who is the legal commander. In the event of incapacitation of the captain, the first officer will assume command of*

> the aircraft.

> Control of the aircraft is normally shared equally between the first officer and the captain, with one pilot normally designated the "Pilot Flying" (PF) and the other the "Pilot Not Flying" (PNF), or "Pilot Monitoring" (PM), for each flight. Even when the first officer is the flying pilot, however, the captain remains ultimately responsible for the aircraft, its passengers, and the crew. In typical day-to-day operations, the essential job tasks remain fairly equal."

> I've always liked the dynamic on the Star Trek series between Captains and First Officers. It's always been quite apparent that the First Officer is always competent and skilled, and if anything happens to the Captain, they step into the role of being in command immediately. The Captain always listens, sometimes the First Officer has a better idea than their own. Sometimes the First Officer actually overrules the Captain in a crisis and gives the crew an order, the Captain usually just trusts the First Officer isn't doing this to make trouble and runs with it. But at the end of the day... the Captain is the Captain and leadership comes from them, and final responsibility for the ship lies with them. If it all goes to hell the Captain is last off the ship.

> My realization is that most wives want the First Officer job. Not Crewman Third Class, but not Captain either. They want to have a say and be heard, they want to be trusted, they don't want to be micro-managed on decisions they are capable of making themselves, they can happily step it up into "having the bridge" when their husbands aren't available. They just would rather be the second in command and follow someone else's leadership and general direction.[1]

This is a great picture of the Biblical Order in action. Here are a few verses that will help you get a better picture of what being a

Captain in your marriage should look like:

> *Husbands, love your wives, just as Christ loved the church and gave himself up for her.*
> *- Ephesians 5:25 (NIV)*
>
> *Husbands, love your wives and do not be harsh with them.*
> *- Colossians 3:19 (NIV)*
>
> *Husbands, in the same way be considerate as you live with your wives, and treat them with respect as the weaker partner and as heirs with you of the gracious gift of life…*
> *- 1 Peter 3:7 (NIV)*

The Bible clearly instructs men not to abuse their position of authority. A husband is to love his wife as Christ loved the church. And how did Christ love the church? By putting the needs of the church above His own.

As Captain, you should be ready and willing to sacrifice even your very life for your First Officer if it comes to that. That's a pretty tall order. You'll want to make sure you are prepared to accept this job position before you sign on the dotted line. You'll also want to be certain that you've got a First Officer worthy of the calling. More on that later.

As First Officer, a woman has a different set of instructions to follow. Her role is to submit to the leadership of the Captain:

> *Wives, submit to your husbands as to the Lord. For the husband is the head of the wife as Christ is the head of the church, his body, of which he is the Savior. Now as the church submits to Christ, so also wives should submit to their husbands in everything.*
> *- Ephesians 5:22-24 (NIV)*
>
> *Wives, submit to your husbands, as is fitting in the Lord.*
> *- Colossians 3:18 (NIV)*

> *Wives, in the same way be submissive to your husbands so that, if any of them do not believe the word, they may be won over without words by the behavior of their wives.*
> *- 1 Peter 3:1 (NIV)*

The pattern in both of these lists is unmistakable. Husbands are to love their wives, and wives are to submit to their husbands. There is certainly room for flexibility and mutual submission, but at the end of the day the Captain is still the Captain. They are two halves of the same whole, but that whole has a hierarchy:

> *In the Lord, however, woman is not independent of man, nor is man independent of woman. For as woman came from man, so also man is born of woman. But everything comes from God.*
> *- 1 Corinthians 11:11-12 (NIV)*

> *Now I want you to realize that the head of every man is Christ, and the head of the woman is man, and the head of Christ is God.*
> *- 1 Corinthians 11:3 (NIV)*

As we'll see later, this arrangement is not only biblical, it's also instinctive. Whether they realize it or not, most men want to be Captain and most women want to be First Officer. God has encoded this blueprint right into our emotional DNA, and when we allow things to work as God intended we will find that they actually work a lot better than when we try to do them our own way.

---

[1] http://marriedmansexlife.com/2010/03/dominance-and-submission-in-marriage-the-captain-and-first-officer-model/

Chapter Four
Complementary Natures

So, we see that there is Biblical Order, and that Christian marriage contains a chain of command in which the husband submits to God and the wife submits to both God and her husband.

Because He knew that men and women would have different roles, God created them with different, but complementary, natures:

> *But at the beginning of creation God 'made them male and female.' For this reason a man will leave his father and mother and be united to his wife, and the two will become one flesh. So they are no longer two, but one.*
> *- Mark 10:6-8 (NIV)*

Men and women, in case you've never noticed, are different in a great many ways. Men are typically bigger and physically stronger than women, with a greater capacity for logical thinking. Women are typically smaller and physically weaker than men, with a greater capacity for emotional thinking.

These complementary traits are perfectly suited for the unique challenges that men and women face throughout their lives.

Historically, men have been responsible for providing the bulk of the food, as well as protecting their families. A large frame and strong upper body are ideal for hunting wild animals, performing hard labor and fighting off potential enemies.

Women, in contrast, have historically been in charge of maintaining the home and family. Cooking, cleaning, sewing, nurturing the children – all of these were necessary functions and a family could not survive without somebody doing them.

You can see, then, the great wisdom of creating men and women with complementary natures. It was, in reality, a gift to humanity because it provided men and women with the opportunity to team up with someone who had a skill set that contained all the tools their own was lacking.

The two parts became one whole. And, not coincidentally, this also provided the ideal environment for raising children with both biological parents present and involved – which study after study has confirmed is the best arrangement for raising happy, well-balanced kids.[1]

God's design for families is a closed, interdependent ring which is often called the "nuclear family". The husband needs the wife, the wife needs the husband and the kids need both of their parents.

This was the way God designed things to work. Did people still struggle? Of course. Did people sometimes take advantage of the system? You bet. But, on the whole, this design has served mankind extremely well throughout the years.

By working together as a team, husbands and wives were able to maximize their strengths and minimize their weaknesses. Eventually, as civilization grew, this arrangement evolved into an unwritten agreement between the sexes which can be thought of as a societal contract.

People understood that, without a division of male and female roles, society would crumble beneath them all. Therefore, men were not only expected to be the breadwinners and protectors of their own families, but they were expected, as a group, to look out for all women and children in society. Women, in turn, deferred to the men and followed their lead.

We will explore the societal contract in greater detail in later chapters. However, this, in a nutshell, was the unspoken agreement between women and men in almost all cultures throughout history.

Chapter Five
The Rebellion Against God's Order

God's design for inter-gender relations has served humanity well. Following His design, we have achieved things that would have seemed mere fantasy to people in ancient times.

Computers, automobiles, modern medicine – even Western civilization itself – all of these things became possible as men and women worked together within the framework of the societal contract that evolved from God's Order.

Western civilization, however, has begun to turn its back on this order. We have adopted a "Progressive" ideology which is completely at odds with God's design. It began with a simple questioning of the established order, but has now blossomed into an outright rebellion against it.

Progressives believe that individual autonomy is the ultimate good, and therefore anything that gets in the way of that autonomy is seen as an evil that must be eradicated. This idea has permeated the West in many areas, but for our purposes we shall focus on only one aspect: gender roles.

[Progressivism] is one of the most radical of ideologies as it is based on a single, overriding good which society is expected to conform to.

Liberals would describe that good as "freedom" or perhaps as "equal freedom" but they mean something very specific by this. They mean that the individual should be unimpeded in self-defining, or self-creating, or self-determining their existence, in other words, that the individual should be autonomous.

That sounds appealing, but when it is made the sole organizing good of society, it has exceptionally radical outcomes.

It means that anything that we cannot self-determine is looked on negatively as an impediment to our freedom.

What can't we self-determine? We do not get to choose which sex we are. Therefore, liberals are forced to conclude that our sex should be made not to matter. The liberal future is a unisex one, in which men and women are expected to live undifferentiated lives.

That's why gender equality in a liberal state is not thought of as 'equal but different' or as 'equal with complementary roles' but as 'equal with the same roles'. Where roles continue to differ it is assumed to be the product of sexism or discrimination and the state intervenes with policies or laws to overcome the situation.

There are liberals who even question the reality of sex distinctions. They believe that the distinction between male and female is a social construct rather than a natural reality. For instance, Professor Judith Butler has written that,

> *... gender is a performance ... Because there is neither an "essence" that gender expresses or*

> externalizes nor an objective ideal to which gender aspires; because gender is not a fact, the various acts of gender create the idea of gender, and without those acts, there would be no gender at all. Gender is, thus, a construction...

Similarly, an influential Australian academic, Dr. Michael Flood believes that we should not,

> take as given the categories of "men" and "women". The binaries of male and female are socially produced ...

The Swedish government has made it official state policy that sex distinctions are nothing more than social constructs. Jens Orback, a government minister, declared that,

> The government considers female and male as social constructions, that means gender patterns are created by upbringing, culture, economic conditions, power structures and political ideologies.

Another Swedish state official, Monica Silvell, followed up by noting that as a result of the new thinking in her country,

> The old view of men and women complementing one another was replaced by the notion that the sexes were basically similar.[1]

As you can see, Progressives of all stripes are united in a concerted effort to break down the Biblical Order and make gender no longer matter. They see men and women as interchangeable units, so traditional gender roles are seen as a hindrance to social progress.

Feminism, in particular, has been detrimental to traditional gender roles. Most women identify with feminism on at least some level, and feminists often claim to represent the collective interests of women as a whole. However, in many cases, the goals of feminism and the desires of most women are diametrically opposed.

It was feminists who insisted that women wanted to get out of the house and into the workforce, yet, in spite of their great progress in the working world, women are actually less happy now than they were before feminism:

> *Women are less happy nowadays despite 40 years of feminism, a new study claims. Despite having more opportunities than ever before, they have a lower sense of well-being and life satisfaction, it found.*
>
> *The study,* The Paradox of Declining Female Happiness, *said the same was true for women of different ages and whether or not they were married or had children. It said the results appeared surprising given that modern women had been liberated from their traditional 1950s role of housewife.*
>
> *Instead, their earning power has soared, women are doing better than men in education and they are in control of decisions over whether to start a family. The findings were released as Sir Stuart Rose, chairman of Marks & Spencer, claimed that women 'have never had it so good'.*[2]

In fact, recent polls show that most women would prefer to be home with their kids rather than working to help support the family financially:

> *Three out of four new mothers would stay at home to bring up their child if they could afford to, a report said yesterday. A traditional family – with a breadwinning father and a full-time mother – remains the ideal for the vast majority of women, the study found.*
>
> *The conclusion flies in the face of the assumption among politicians, civil servants and academics that working is good for mothers and that what families really want is more*

> *subsidized childcare. According to the research, six out of ten mothers who return to work after having a baby do so only to pay off debt or ease financial pressures. Just one in seven said they wanted to develop their career.*
>
> *The findings, produced from a survey commissioned by uSwitch of 1,008 mothers, back up a series of opinion polls in recent years, all of which showed that a high proportion of new mothers would prefer to stay at home.*[3]

So, despite decades of Progressive policies and "liberation", it turns out the majority of women still prefer a traditional household where the husband works while the wife maintains the home and raises their children.

Unfortunately, feminism has created a world in which, for most women anyway, working outside the home is no longer optional but necessary. This result was not accidental, but deliberate:

> *"No woman should be authorized to stay home to raise her children. Society should be totally different. Women should not have that choice precisely because if there is such a choice, too many women would make that one."*
> *- Simone de Beauvoir*

The ultimate goal of Progressives, whether conscious or subconscious, is a complete breakdown of God's Order. And because our entire societal contract rests upon that foundation, their rebellion has thrown a monkey wrench into the very heart of our civilization.

Men and women no longer know what is expected of them in society because they are constantly being bombarded by mixed messages.

Men are now told to be chivalrous, but only when women want them to be. A young man should be prepared to pay on a date, for instance, even though young women now often earn more money than young men.[4] And, in the case of a military draft, he will be expected to enlist while his female peers won't be. Yet, he'll also be told that actions such as holding a door for a woman or offering to carry something heavy are sexist actions because they reinforce gender stereotypes:

> *Men who open doors for women are guilty of 'benevolent sexism' according to a new study by feminist psychologists. Helping the ladies choose the right computer as well as carrying their shopping are also signs of 'unseen' sexism in society, according to the report.*
>
> ...
>
> *Even though they are not aware of it, such regular and daily sexism only reinforces inequality and injustice, it is argued.*[5]

Women, on the other hand, are told that they are chock full of moxie and better than men at pretty much everything.[6] Yet, they have their own sports leagues and receive a head start during marathon races[7] because, when they have to compete physically with men on a level playing field, most of them simply can't keep up.

These and other contradictions between our societal contract and our Progressive culture make finding your place in today's world a very challenging prospect for both men and women.

---

1 http://ozconservative.blogspot.com/2011/05/devouring-ideology.html

2 http://www.dailymail.co.uk/femail/article-1189894/Women-happy-years-ago-.html

3 http://www.dailymail.co.uk/news/article-2199539/75-new-mothers-stay-home-bring-child-afford-to.html

4 http://www.time.com/time/business/article/0,8599,2015274,00.html

5 http://www.dailymail.co.uk/news/article-2003821/Feminists-claim-men-hold-open-doors-women-SEXIST-chivalrous.html

6 http://www.glamour.com/sex-love-life/2011/02/women-are-better-than-men

7 http://www.nytimes.com/2008/03/03/sports/othersports/03run.html

Chapter Six
A World Without Bicycles

I've said before that this is more than just a drifting away from God's Order – it's an outright rebellion against it. This is not mere hyperbole. We have gone from a hierarchy where men were seen as the leaders in society to a hierarchy where men are considered to be little better than dogs:

> *"The male is a domestic animal which, if treated with firmness and kindness, can be trained to do most things."*
> *- Jilly Cooper*

This quote sums up the modern view of men in a single sentence. Where once men were seen as innovators, thinkers and protectors, they are now seen as barely even human – throwbacks to a simpler time, knuckle-dragging Neanderthals who would pull the world down into the mud without women around to civilize and direct them.

Never mind, of course, that civilization was built, and is mostly maintained, by men:

> *It is men who have built the houses, the bridges, the roads, the*

> *railways, the dams, the factories, the ships, the canals, the monuments, the airports, the churches, the offices, the tunnels, the engines, the industrial machinery etc. ...*
>
> *It is men mostly who have worked in the factories, the furnaces, the sewers, the mines etc...*
>
> *It is men mostly who have, rightly or wrongly, fought the wars, fought the crimes, fought the elements, fought the odds etc. ...*
>
> *And it is men who have invented, discovered and done just about everything that has ever been invented, discovered and done.*[1]

It is in this context that I would like to examine the notion, made popular by Gloria Steinem, that a woman needs a man like a fish needs a bicycle.

If men are indeed simple brutes, lumbering animals capable of producing things of value only under the watchful supervision of a woman, then it would logically follow that the world would be just fine without them.

A cursory glance at history, however, turns this notion on its head in double-quick time. The greatest scientists[2], mathematicians[3], artists[4], philosophers[5], musicians[6] and writers[7] throughout all of history have almost exclusively been male. The exceptions prove the rule.

It *is* true that, thanks to the largely male-created technological wonderland we call Western civilization, it is now possible for a woman to live comfortably on her own without a man in her life. So in that sense, no, she does not need a man.

But it's also clear that men are vital to the underlying structure of the society upon which her lifestyle depends, so she very much does still need men in general.

What's happened, though, is that women have forgotten that it was men who made Western civilization possible in the first place, and it's men who do most of the dangerous and dirty jobs that keep it all going.[8]

Men, as a group, have become the collective butt of the joke as women imply that they are no longer necessary to society, and this is largely responsible for the rapidly burgeoning exodus of men away from the unwritten contract that holds civilization together.

As we've already seen, the societal contract states that men as a group will always protect women as a group. You could call this the *Bicycle Clause*. It dictates that a woman without a man of her own, either temporarily or permanently, may procure assistance from a nearby man without any prior relationship existing between them or any expectation of reciprocation.

This clause can be invoked for anything from changing a tire to intervening in a violent situation. Simply put, any man must be ready to risk life and limb to protect any woman, even one he doesn't know, at a moment's notice. A man who saves a woman's life is seen as a hero while a man who chooses not to get involved is seen as a coward.

A well-worn but fantastic example of the *Bicycle Clause* in action was the sinking of the Titanic in 1912. The men onboard knew there weren't enough lifeboats for everyone, yet they willingly remained on a sinking ship to allow the women and children a chance to escape an icy death.

This was considered proper and good by everyone involved and by society in general:

> *English Suffragettes of prominence, when questioned as to what they thought of the men who died on the Titanic in order that women might be saved, seem to have manifested a disposition, possibly significant, almost to resent the*

> *inquirer's obvious belief that the display of chivalry was magnificent.*
>
> *While the strenuous ladies did not deny that the behavior of the men was rather fine, they hinted that after all it only fulfilled a plain duty and therefore had not earned any particularly enthusiastic praise.*[9]

The men on Titanic did what they did because it was understood that women were weaker than men, and were therefore in need of protection. Men, on the other hand, were generally expected to take care of themselves.

But, if women are at least equal (if not superior) to men, then this part of the contract no longer applies. To demand equality is to renounce the clause in the contract that grants special privileges based on a presumption of weakness.

Yet, despite our modern society's insistence that women should be treated no differently than men, the notion persists that men should selflessly put women they don't even know ahead of themselves:

> *One of the features of the [Costa Concordia] disaster that has provoked a great deal of comment is the stream of reports from angry survivors of how, in the chaos, men refused to put women and children first, and instead pushed themselves forward to escape.*[10]

But you simply can't have it both ways. This is a binary question with only two possible answers – either women are weaker than men and need their protection, or they are equally capable and they do not.

Currently, the cultural directive is that women are just as capable as men, therefore men are responding by letting women fend for themselves. To blame men for looking out for their own interests when they have been taught that women don't want or need their help is not only counter-productive, it's grossly unfair as well.

To put it plainly, in a world where bicycles are no longer desired, none will be produced. It's simple supply and demand. Women are, by their words and actions, saying that they are fish who no longer need bicycles, and are therefore creating for themselves a world without them.

Let's just hope that if (and when) women find themselves wishing they had a bicycle, they realize the reason they don't have one is that they collectively insisted they didn't need one.

1 http://www.angryharry.com/esLikeAFishNeedsABicycle.htm

2 http://www.adherents.com/people/100_scientists.html

3 http://fabpedigree.com/james/mathmen.htm

4 http://www.theartwolf.com/articles/most-important-painters.htm

5 http://listverse.com/2011/02/19/top-10-greatest-philosophers-in-history/

6 http://blogs.laweekly.com/westcoastsound/2012/01/top_20_musicians_of_all_time_complete_list.php

7 http://thisrecording.com/today/2009/8/3/in-which-these-are-the-100-greatest-writers-of-all-time.html

8 http://www.aei-ideas.org/2011/09/next-equal-occupational-fatality-day-due-october-2021/

9 http://query.nytimes.com/gst/abstract.html?res=F20611FE3E5813738DDDA00994DC405B828DF1D3

10 http://www.dailymail.co.uk/debate/article-2087585/Cruise-ship-Costa-Concordia-sinking-Whatever-happened-women-children-first.html

Chapter Seven
On Civilization, Feminism and "Manning Up"

If civilization is a machine, then men are the fuel that makes it run. From the simplest hunter-gatherer community to the most complex world superpower, it is men who make civilized society possible.

It is men who wrestle control of the land away from the wild beasts and tame rugged terrain to create roads and cities. It is men who fight to earn and subsequently protect territory. And it is men, mostly, who do the dirty and thankless jobs required to keep the ship of civilization afloat.

The primary reason that men join together in all these endeavors – indeed one of the reasons that living in an advanced society is an appealing prospect to them in the first place – is that having a society allows more men to participate in fatherhood:

> *You see, all throughout the animal kingdom, motherhood is a pretty common theme. It is positively everywhere! What is not common in the animal kingdom however, is fatherhood.*

> *Nope, not too many baby deer know who their fathers are. Fatherhood is a foreign concept in most of the animal kingdom.*
>
> *Female mammals often find themselves living in a herd filled with many other females, all being bred by one dominant alpha male. The females congregate in herds because it is the only way they and their offspring can safely survive.*
>
> *…*
>
> *But, one must wonder, what happens to the males that don't become the alpha male who breeds the whole lot of women? Well, when a male reaches sexual maturity, he must challenge for breeding rights within the herd. Those males who fail to successfully challenge the alpha males become beta males, and get forced to leave the herd by the alpha. The beta males generally end up living on the fringes of the herd/society where they fend for themselves individually.[1]*

So, if the inability to raise their own offspring is the defining characteristic of most males in the animal kingdom, then it is literally the concept of marriage that separates us from the animals.

> *Remember all those beta males who were existing outside of the herd, living on the fringes of society? They were only exerting 20-30% of their potential labor to survive.*
> *Once married and attached to their own children, these beta males were suddenly yoked like an ox and working at 100% capacity. This utilization of the full capacity of male labor is what pulled mankind into a civilization. It is what built our houses and planted our corn. It built our roads and our bridges. It created our literature and our art. It created, well, pretty much everything that we have. Men, women and children all obviously benefited from this.[1]*

Historically, when a man and a woman entered into a marriage contract, it provided the man with an opportunity to raise children of his own, and it provided the woman care and protection for herself and the children which she would bear to the man. This is the bedrock of civilization.

As we've already discussed, men do the vast majority of the heavy lifting in every civilization, literally as well as figuratively. The system that naturally arose out of this arrangement is one based largely on hierarchy.

A doctor commands more respect than a garbage collector, for example, because being a doctor takes more training and requires a keener mind. Similarly, a general commands more respect than a foot soldier because he has put in his time and has earned a position of honor.

Ok, are you still with me? Good. Now that we've established the groundwork I'm going to shift gears and open up the throttle a bit.

So, here we have Western civilization. The industrial revolution has been a huge success and life is getting easier for both men and women all the time. Things are humming along nicely, with the men going into the workplace to carve out a living for themselves and their families while their wives are maintaining the home and nurturing the children. The system is working as intended.

But along comes Progressivism, which claims that pre-determined gender roles are oppressive, and says we should instead be striving to be completely autonomous individuals.

Feminists begin telling women that they have been oppressed by the men of society. Suddenly, many women feel that they've been given the short end of the stick, and somehow it's unfair that they are stuck toiling in the home while their husbands are out toiling at a job.

In an effort to right these perceived wrongs, society changes the rules in the middle of the game. Now, women can choose to either be stay-at-home-moms or climb the corporate ladder right alongside the men.

It must be pointed out here that there have always been some women in the workforce. Women in the workforce didn't come about as a result of feminism; rather, feminism changed the culture's view of working women and encouraged more of them to seek careers of their own as a way to maximize their autonomy.

Prior to feminism, a woman's natural sphere was in the home with the children. Most women who worked outside the home did so only out of necessity. By pushing women into the workforce en masse, feminism altered the structure of our civilization in some fundamental ways.

One of the primary effects of feminism was a disruption of the hierarchy. Women wanted to work because they desired respect and fulfillment, but you don't get either of those from being a plumber. On top of that, women simply aren't as good at jobs that require upper body strength or great physical exertion.[2]

So, we had an influx of women heading straight for the cleanest, most comfortable and highest paying middle class jobs on the market:

> *Women are beginning to pour into management and professional occupations that require more education and offer higher pay and status. In fact, women are now dominating some of the jobs that used to belong to men, according to the Department of Labor's Women's Bureau.*[3]

This has resulted in a large group of middle class men who are losing access to the better mid-range jobs because there simply aren't enough of them to go around. The only jobs women are leaving many of these men are the dirty, difficult and low-status jobs that women can't (or don't want to) do themselves.

Yet, as we've already seen, women are actually less happy now than they were before feminism. Despite holding many of the best middle class jobs society has to offer, the vast majority would prefer to be back at home raising their own children:

> *According to a new partnered survey cosponsored by ForbesWoman and TheBump.com, a growing number of women see staying home to raise children (while a partner provides financial support) to be the ideal circumstances of motherhood. Forget the corporate climb; these young mothers have another definition of success: setting work aside to stay home with the kids.*
>
> …
>
> *It's true: according to our survey, 84% of working women told ForbesWoman and TheBump that staying home to raise children is a financial luxury they aspire to. What's more, more than one in three resent their partner for not earning enough to make that dream a reality.[4]*

What an appalling indictment of feminism! The very social changes that were supposed to liberate women from oppression have forced most of them to live a lifestyle they wouldn't otherwise have chosen for themselves. Who's really being oppressive?

What's more, many of these same women still believe that feminists generally speak on their behalf. They don't realize the damage that is being done to their own personal lives by these radical Progressives; indeed many blame their own husbands for their inability to overcome a system that is stacked against them.

But the disruption to our culture doesn't end here. In addition to pushing women into the workforce, feminists also insisted that women should be able to have socially approved sex outside of marriage.

The sexual revolution ushered in sweeping changes to the way our culture views sex:

> *By the 1960s, the conviction that sexual expression was healthy and good—the more of it, the better—and that sexual desire was intrinsic to one's personal identity culminated in the sexual revolution, the animating spirit of which held that freedom and authenticity were to be found not in sexual withholding (the Christian view) but in sexual expression and assertion.*[5]

But, in spite of all the "sex positive" messages, there is still a stigma associated with women who engage in uncommitted sex. This remains a point of contention among Progressives. Why is it that a man who has sex with many women is considered to be a stud, while a woman who has sex with many men is shamed as a slut?

Well, for one thing, it's a lot more difficult for a man to acquire sex than it is for a woman. Women are the gatekeepers of sex while men, in contrast, are the gatekeepers of commitment.

Pretty much any woman could walk into a bar and announce that she wanted to have sex and men would be lining up in seconds. A man who did the same thing would receive nothing but empty stares and, perhaps, a few chuckles.

But there's actually an even deeper reason that women are shamed for playing fast and loose with their sexuality. Let's take another look at our budding civilization:

> *You see, the feminists always leave out that the woman sold her sexuality and took something in exchange for it: The man's surplus labor. And benefit from a man's surplus labor the wives of the past most surely did!*

> *She benefited by no longer having to rely on the Communist lifestyle of the herd for her survival. When in need of protection she pushed the man out the door first to deal with the danger, rather than rely on the size of the herd, hoping it would hide her from harm when the weak stragglers get taken down by the wolves.*
>
> *She benefited enormously by increasing the amount of labor available to her, giving her the ability to live in a wooden house with a real roof, rather than sharing a grass hut with a bunch of other women.*
>
> *Women took something very real in exchange for selling their sexuality. They took a man's labor as their own, and they benefited from this in almost every way imaginable. So did the children she mothered benefit a great deal, and so did society in general.*[1]

The societal contract states that men will work hard to keep the civilization going and protect the women and children around them. That's their end of the bargain.

The reason that single women are ostracized for their sexual exploits while men aren't is that, according to the contract, young women should be providing young men an opportunity to get married and have children. By sleeping around in her fertile years, rather than settling down with one man, a woman is essentially thumbing her nose at the contract that makes the very society she lives in possible.

Nevertheless, the casual dating scene continues to expand as more and more empowered young women choose short-term flings over long-term relationships:

> *Single young women in their sexual prime—that is, their 20s and early 30s … are for the first time in history more successful, on average, than the single young men around them. They are more likely to have a college degree and, in*

> *aggregate, they make more money. What makes this remarkable development possible is not just the pill or legal abortion but the whole new landscape of sexual freedom—the ability to delay marriage and have temporary relationships that don't derail education or career. To put it crudely, feminist progress right now largely depends on the existence of the hookup culture. And to a surprising degree, it is women—not men—who are perpetuating the culture, especially in school, cannily manipulating it to make space for their success, always keeping their own ends in mind. For college girls these days, an overly serious suitor fills the same role an accidental pregnancy did in the 19th century: a danger to be avoided at all costs, lest it get in the way of a promising future.[6]*

This system seems to offer women the best of both worlds – casual sex now and marriage later. However, this all rests on the assumption that men will always be standing by, ready to fulfill their traditional male responsibilities when the women decide that they are finally ready for a serious relationship.

What many of these women are discovering, however, is that a growing number of men are no longer following the script:

> *At this point, certainly, falling in love and getting married may be less a matter of choice than a stroke of wild great luck. A decade ago, luck didn't even cross my mind. I'd been in love before, and I'd be in love again.*
>
> …
>
> *We took for granted that we'd spend our 20s finding ourselves, whatever that meant, and save marriage for after we'd finished graduate school and launched our careers, which of course would happen at the magical age of 30. That we would marry, and that there would always be men we wanted to marry, we took on faith.*

...

> *But what transpired next lay well beyond the powers of everybody's imagination: as women have climbed ever higher, men have been falling behind. We've arrived at the top of the staircase, finally ready to start our lives, only to discover a cavernous room at the tail end of a party, most of the men gone already, some having never shown up—and those who remain are leering by the cheese table, or are, you know, the ones you don't want to go out with.*[7]

What nobody stopped to consider was that modifications to our societal contract do not take place in a vacuum. A change that effectively rewards men who are good prospects for short term flings while penalizing men who are good prospects for marriage will produce more men who are focused on the short term rather than the long term. To put it bluntly, incentives matter:

> *Men in their age group aren't getting as strong a signal that working hard to become a provider will result in a long term relationship and later marriage ... [therefore] a significant percentage of men haven't felt the incentive to prepare themselves as a provider.*
>
> *Even worse, these [career women] pushed out men from their slots in school and the workplace. So the men they one day hope to marry both have less incentive to do the extra work and planning to become a provider and face additional obstacles to do so.*[8]

And so, because of these cultural changes, it seems that young men have begun to shirk their societal duties. Rather than putting their shoulders to the plow, many men are choosing instead to fill their time with pursuits of leisure and fun:

> *The statistic from Bennett's book that perhaps struck me the most is that teenage boys, ages 12-to-17 years old, actually spend less time playing video games than 18-to-34-year-old*

> men. I can understand the desire to play a video game here and there as a kid, but as an adult? Grow up.
>
> These men should be studying in college, getting a job, and contributing to society through the workforce and family. How in the world do they have time to play video games for hours? The answer is that they just don't ever grow up.[9]

But what social commentators don't understand is that these "Peter Pan Men" aren't really shirking their duties at all. They are simply joining the exodus of women returning to the old pre-contract system.

Prior to the contract, you will recall, a young male only expended about 30% of his energy to create a life for himself. The only reason these beta males started giving 100% in the first place was because it was in their own best interest to do so.

Under the societal contract, getting married and working his tail off was the only way for a young man to gain socially approved access to sex and, by extension, a positive male identity through his role as a husband and father.

But things are different now. By incentivizing men to focus on short term happiness through easy sexual access, we have essentially raised a generation of men who have no reason to work hard in life.

It's easy to point the finger at these men and complain that they are being lazy; however, this will ultimately get us nowhere. Because we have embraced the idea that a modern woman should be autonomous, choosing whatever lifestyle best suits her own personal aspirations, we have no choice but make the same acquiescence for the modern man. Equality cuts both ways.

According to the pre-contract rules, as long as a man is pulling his own weight he doesn't owe society a darn thing. If he wants to scrape by with a menial job and spend all his free time playing video games then that is his choice to make. It's only the societal contract that says men ought to be doing more than the bare minimum, and women are the ones who shredded it – not men.

Of course, the rub is this: society needs men to continue doing what they've always done or the civilization will fail. A civilization can chug along, however poorly, with women not holding up their end of the contract, so long as the men keep holding up theirs.

But if the men abandon their posts, then it's game over. Deep down everyone knows this is true. That's why commentators are cranking out "man up" articles like there's no tomorrow – because if men, as a group, suddenly decide that the rat race just isn't worth it anymore – *there won't be.*

1 http://no-maam.blogspot.com/2008/02/questionators-should-women-have-right.html

2 http://www.military.com/military-fitness/army-fitness-requirements/army-basic-training-pft

3 http://www.forbes.com/sites/jennagoudreau/2011/03/07/20-surprising-jobs-women-are-taking-over/

4 http://www.forbes.com/sites/meghancasserly/2012/09/12/is-opting-out-the-new-american-dream-for-working-women/

5 http://www.theamericanconservative.com/articles/sex-after-christianity/

6 http://www.theatlantic.com/magazine/archive/2012/09/boys-on-the-side/309062/

7 http://www.theatlantic.com/magazine/archive/2011/11/all-the-single-ladies/308654/

8 http://dalrock.wordpress.com/2011/11/25/playing-career-woman/

9 http://www.foxnews.com/opinion/2011/10/07/why-does-america-have-so-many-peter-pan-men/

Chapter Eight
Rediscovering Masculinity

Today's young men have clearly lost their way. Without a societal contract to define gender roles, we don't even know what being a man means in our current society. And because we have no definition of manhood, our culture has begun to view manhood as an extension of womanhood.

Modern men are often portrayed as under-evolved women – bumbling brutes who, with proper training and encouragement, can overcome their primal testosterone-driven urges to become almost fully human:

> *"The male chromosome is an incomplete female chromosome. In other words the male is a walking abortion; aborted at the gene stage. To be male is to be deficient, emotionally limited; maleness is a deficiency disease and males are emotional cripples."*
> - Valerie Solanas

The assault on maleness begins in childhood. Impetuous masculinity is seen as a character flaw that must be stamped out at all costs. We are raising boys in a world that discourages adventure in favor of entertainment and exchanges risk for safety. Boys with stronger wills who aren't as easily steered into passivity are simply drugged into a state of complacency.[1]

As a result, the rugged masculinity that built this country is fading into the memory hole as more and more young men enter adulthood without any knowledge whatsoever of what it means to be a man. They are drifting through our egalitarian utopia where men and women are considered to be exactly the same, wondering why they feel so empty inside.

As these young men wander aimlessly through life, they slowly begin to adapt to the world with which they are presented. With no inspiration and no cause to unite them, many men are simply dropping out of the rat race and into lives of sterile mediocrity. Others marry but are unhappy anyway because their role as a husband and father is seen by society as extraneous (if not completely unnecessary) and their wives treat them as if they don't even matter.

What these men all have in common is that they are sick and tired of the lot they've inherited. They are beginning to realize that, under the current system, they are being used as expendable pawns to prop up a decaying social system that demands their participation while providing few benefits in return for their efforts:

> *All of the approved paths to a positive male identity, the paths society endorses and depends on, are gone. Even when men don't consciously realize it, they know it somewhere in the backs of their brains.*
>
> *Men have always been willing to work and sacrifice and sweat and bleed if they were rewarded with a means through which to see themselves as worthy of respect. But when every single role society wants to cram you into is no longer a way to respect yourself, or have the respect of others, then it's*

> *really time to throw those roles away.*
>
> *And the thing that [those at the top of society] are never going to realize is that using shame to try to coerce men to do what is expected of them isn't going to work this time.*
>
> ...
>
> *When the cost of society's approval is the self-respect you derive from a positive identity, it ceases to be worth it to a lot of men.*[2]

You see, because our civilization has abandoned the societal contract, today's young men have been left no choice but to reinvent themselves. Feminism changed what it means to be a woman; therefore it has, by extension, changed what it means to be a man. Masculinity is due for an overhaul, and men are beginning to rise to the challenge.

Thanks to the internet, men all over the world are connecting in ways that would have been impossible just a few years ago. They are discovering that they are not crazy and that being a man is not so terrible after all. Websites like *The Art of Manliness* are booming as young men discover that masculinity is actually a good thing.

In some cases, this rediscovery of masculinity is bringing about a rebirth of traditional masculine identity. However, in many others, the form that masculinity is taking is a whole new animal, no longer restricted by the societal contract of the past.

Because of this split, going forward, manhood will no longer be defined solely by how it benefits women or society in general, just as womanhood is no longer defined solely in terms of being a housewife and raising children. From now on, each man will define manhood for himself.

This is why shaming men no longer works like it once did. You can only shame somebody who believes that they are under an obligation to do what you say, and many of today's young men simply don't identify with the traditional male gender role. They are men, yes, but they are *autonomous* men who are creating their own script in life – just like women have been doing for decades.

This à la carte masculinity will undoubtedly result in more options and personal freedom for individual men than they would have had under the old system. But, as with feminism, these newfound freedoms will almost certainly come at a cost to society as a whole.

Whatever comes of this masculine awakening, it must be remembered that men did not choose this path for themselves; they merely responded to a system that had already discarded traditional gender roles to begin with.

---

1 http://www.webmd.com/add-adhd/childhood-adhd/news/20040915/study-confirms-adhd-is-more-common-in-boys

2 http://www.youtube.com/watch?v=rlvMAS_20K4

Chapter Nine
Alpha Beta Soup

Now that you have a basic understanding of God's Order and the societal contract, we can finally start discussing what modern marriage is and why it's so challenging. And believe me, modern marriage *is* challenging.

With the societal contract in disarray, we have entered an unstable new landscape in which simply being a nice guy and working hard are no longer enough to gain (or keep) a wife.

Back in the old days, people would often get married right out of high school. A young man would get a job and begin working his way up the career ladder while his wife would get busy turning their modest house into a home. Society itself did a pretty good job getting couples together and keeping them together for the long haul.

But, unfortunately, things are not so simple anymore. With sex outside of marriage now openly encouraged and a strong cultural push toward women having careers of their own, the dynamics of courtship have changed dramatically.

You are going to need a set of tools if you want to land yourself a wife, and those tools are called "Game":

> At its root level, Game is a series of behavioural modifications to life skills based on psychological and sociological principles to facilitate intersexual relations between genders.[1]

There are a lot of misconceptions about Game out there, so let me give you an analogy to help you understand what Game is – and what it isn't.

For this analogy let's assume that you want to be a college professor. Now, some people have the gift of gab. They are confident, entertaining, and people naturally listen to what they have to say. But you are shy. You lack that natural charisma. What do you do?

You get yourself some books about public speaking. You watch other people speaking in public to see how they carry themselves. You teach yourself pacing and tone. You practice avoiding words like "ah" and "um" when you speak. You train yourself to be clear and direct while maintaining eye contact with the people you are addressing.

With enough practice, you will eventually improve your public speaking skills. You may never be a "natural", but the skill set can be mastered by almost anyone who is determined to learn it. Is this trickery? Cheating? Faking? Of course not.

So it is with Game. Game is not a magic ticket that will suddenly make you a ladies' man, but neither is it an act that turns you into some kind of con artist. It's simply a set of skills that can be used to improve your interactions with women.

The core principle of Game is a pair of attributes called "alpha traits" and "beta traits". It's important to understand the difference between these two broad trait categories because everything else in Game hinges on this concept.

You see, women actually have a dual sexual strategy;

subconsciously they are seeking both good genes for their future children and a man who will be a good provider to help raise them.

The male traits that indicate strong genes are the alpha traits, while the traits that indicate that a man would be a good provider are the beta traits. Here are a few examples:

Alpha Traits
Physical Strength
Confidence
Dominance

Beta Traits
Comfort
Reliability
Dependability

An ideal man should have a mix of both sets of traits, but in our culture we have bred the alpha traits right out of most young men. In an effort to tame masculinity, we have raised a whole generation of nice guys who are positively brimming with beta traits but have almost no alpha traits at all.

The problem is that women aren't attracted to men with no alpha traits, no matter how many good beta traits they possess. I know it's difficult to imagine how this could possibly be, so let me give you another analogy to help you see how it works.

Let's say you've got $5,000 and you want to buy a car. You are looking for a car with all six of the following features:

Alpha Features
Fast
Powerful
Fun to drive

Beta Features
Comfortable
Reliable
Gets good gas mileage

But suppose you can't find a car that has both sets of features. Your only choices are a Mustang that has only the alpha features and needs some work, or a pink minivan that has only the beta features and runs great. Which do you choose?

The Mustang of course! Why? Because the Mustang has the traits that attract you to a car in first place. You can work on it as you go and hopefully get it running well sometime down the road.

But buying the minivan is out of the question. Not because it isn't comfortable enough or reliable enough, but because no amount of good beta features can ever make up for the fact that you simply aren't looking for a pink minivan.

That's the situation modern women are facing in today's sexual marketplace. There are basically two kinds of single men out there: nice guys and jerks.

Nice guys have lots of beta traits, and beta traits are important, but they've got no alpha traits so it doesn't matter. Meanwhile, the jerks have lots of alpha traits but no beta traits, which means they are attractive but lack the qualities that would make them good marriage material.

And, just like in our example with the cars, given the choice between a man who is not attractive at all and a man who's attractive but flawed, women are going with the flawed jerks almost every time.

This is why women are always saying there are no good men out there. What they mean is there are no good *alpha* men out there. Alpha traits are what make a man, well, manly. And right now there really is a shortage of good, manly men.

It wasn't always like this, though. There was a time when good men were alpha, too. But, as a society that has rebelled against God's Order, we have stripped good men of their masculine alpha birthright in an effort to make men and women the same.

Nice guys have "gotten in touch with their feminine sides" at the expense of their virile, masculine sides; and they did it precisely because they're the good guys. They were told this was what women wanted in men, so they rebuilt the very foundations of their manhood to give it to them.

But it turns out that men have done precisely the wrong thing. As much as our Progressive society wants to make gender not matter, you simply can't fight biology. At the end of the day, women don't want a feminine man, they want a masculine one. The masculine attracts the feminine just like the feminine attracts the masculine.

Most women are wired to want to follow a man; it is how they were designed. But in order for a woman to want to follow a man she needs to see those masculine alpha traits. Women just are not attracted to a man who has sold his manhood down the river, no matter how noble his intentions.

What it all comes down to is this: in the vast majority of cases, if a man is too heavy on the beta traits and too light on the alpha traits, a woman will not be attracted to him.

Likewise, if a man already in a relationship begins to lean too heavily to the beta side, and he doesn't correct the imbalance by adding some of those alpha qualities back into the mix, he runs the risk of getting some variation of the "I love you, but I'm not *in love* with you" speech.

What she means by this is that she knows she *should* be in love with him, but her biology is being repelled. Her body agenda knows that he is not in a leadership position in the relationship and this is causing her to lose attraction toward him.

Yet, our culture refuses to acknowledge this truth, despite the fact that it's blindingly obvious. Every day, beta men who are struggling in their relationships are told over and over again that they need to be even softer, more supplicating and more comforting.

That's terrible advice. A beta man who is having marriage trouble because of his beta imbalance and then, as a remedy, piles on even more beta is just going to drive his wife further away. The solution is simple:

> *If you're too Beta the solution is to add Alpha. If you're too Alpha, the solution is to add Beta.*[2]

You need a balance. The right balance will depend on your particular woman's temperament and will vary somewhat day to day (most women prefer a little more alpha while ovulating for example[3]), but you still need to have a balance.

For the majority of us, the problem is that we are too beta. We need to add some alpha. Step one is to grow a pair. You are a man; act like one. It's okay to be strong. It's okay to be manly.

Don't strive to be a nice guy – strive to be a good man. Good men have an alpha side. You were designed to be confident and to take the lead. Embrace your natural masculine qualities; I think you'll find they suit you.

---

[1] http://therationalmale.com/2013/04/19/the-evolution-of-game/

[2] http://marriedmansexlife.com/2010/01/the-basics-part-3-the-attraction-switches/

[3] http://www.livescience.com/20294-women-choose-bad-boys.html

Chapter Ten
Shaken, Not Stirred

So, what does a well-balanced man look like? Believe it or not, one of the best examples I know of is Jesus Christ. Not the Jesus you'll see in those paintings where he looks like a Calvin Klein model, but the real one.

Our culture has done a great job of turning Jesus into a soft, non-threatening Savior. This Jesus is all Lamb and no Lion:

> *Jesus was a gaunt, pasty white creature hidden under mounds of flowing robes ... His hair was long, thin, and stringy. He was painted to look strained, tired and supplicant. Gentle Jesus, meek and mild. Soft and suspiciously effeminate. It often seems as if the church is working in collusion with a culture bent on emasculating men and turning raw male material into pliable, defanged images of its own liking.*[1]

Brian Keeper explains:

> *Not only do American teenagers tend to view God as a friendly grandparent who just wants to affirm us all the time,*

> *but they see the point of religion as nothing more than helping us to be "nice" people. And where did they get this view of God and religion? From us adults.*
>
> *The problem with this "Cult of Niceness," as Kendra Creasy Dean notes, is that nice is a "social lubricant," a "cheap and versatile adjective" that "offers a nod without a commitment" (p.33). Nice doesn't let you get mad. Nice doesn't allow you to rightly be outraged in the face of suffering and injustice. Nice sends this message: "Avoid conflict at all cost. Don't rock the boat. Do whatever it takes to get along and be liked, even if truth and justice get shoved aside." Nice smothers the embers of the righteous anger of which St. Paul speaks and leaves behind cool ashes of indifference and apathy.*
>
> *Eugene Peterson puts it this way: "It is in the things that we care about that we are capable of expressing anger. A parent sees a child dart out into a roadway and narrowly miss being hit by a car, and angrily yells at the child, at the driver--at both." This anger (not to be confused with rage) is evidence of concern: "Indifference would be somehow inhuman" (A Long Obedience in the Same Direction, p.127).[2]*

And Jesus did get angry. Not just once, but several times. He also said things that weren't very nice:

> *"You snakes! You brood of vipers! How will you escape being condemned to hell?"*
> *- Matthew 23:33 (NIV)*
>
> *"You unbelieving and perverse generation," Jesus replied, "how long shall I stay with you? How long shall I put up with you?"*
> *- Matthew 17:17 (NIV)*

Jesus was not a "nice guy" – He was a good man. He took care of business when the situation called for it but, at the same time, He was also compassionate, long-suffering and more patient than any mere mortal could ever be. He was alpha but he was also beta. To be one without the other is to be an incomplete man.

Another great example of an alpha/beta man, this one from pop culture, is Jack Dawson from the movie *Titanic*:

> *Jack is more beta on the surface, but he has strong inner game. It is actually this strong inner game that provides the basis for the emotional through-line of the movie. When Jack and Rose first meet, Rose is about to commit suicide by jumping off the back of the ship at night. Jack is able to talk Rose out of suicide using some light negs, nonchalantly reminding her of how cold the water is and how he's [going to have to] jump in to save her, subtly shifting the power in his favor by insinuating that she's being silly and emotional. What he does not do is act like what she's about to do is [serious business]. A lesser man would have acted frightened that Rose would jump.*
>
> *Jack is also unapologetic about his station in life and sees it as a good thing. He does not try to seek Rose's approval (or even make any pledge or attempt to better himself for her). He is unruffled by Cal's continued attempts to belittle him and charms all of Rose's upper-crusty dinner companions. He tells her what to do ("meet me at the clock") rather than requesting behavior of her. He never panics when the ship begins to sink but remains level-headed and provides guidance to Rose the entire time. And (SPOILER ALERT) in the end he does what every woman wishes the man she loves would be willing to do for her: sacrifice his life in order to save hers.*[3]

This, gentlemen, is what you want to strive for. A man takes charge. A man leads. A man does what needs to be done.

Jesus once told a parable about three servants. In the parable, the master of the house gave each servant some money and asked them to invest it while he was out of town:

> *The first two servants invested the money and were rewarded upon the master's return, but the third servant buried the money in the ground. Why? Because he was afraid of what his master would do to him if he invested the money and lost it all.*
>
> *...*
>
> *His master replied, 'You wicked, lazy servant! So you knew that I harvest where I have not sown and gather where I have not scattered seed? Well then, you should have put my money on deposit with the bankers, so that when I returned I would have received it back with interest.*
> *- Matthew 25:24-28 (NIV)*

Building up your alpha/beta balance is going to take some practice and you're going to make mistakes along the way. But God gave you your masculine nature for a reason; you can't just hide from it because you're too fearful to embrace it.

It's time to become the well-balanced man that God intended you to be. This is not an assignment, but an adventure. There are many resources in the back of this book; explore them and they will help you discover the man you were meant to be all along.

1 Paul Coughlin - No More Christian Nice Guy

2 http://www.fellowshipreformed.org/site/interact/blogs/jesus-wasnt-nice-guy

3 http://haleyshalo.wordpress.com/2012/01/05/jack-dawson-game/

Chapter Eleven
Red Pill Dating

So, what exactly is Game? In practice, Game is essentially a reversal of today's typical male mating strategy. Rather than qualifying yourself to women and vying for their attention, you flip the entire script on its head.

You are the one who has high value. *You* are the one who determines who is, and is not, worthy of your time and attention.

Once you understand your true value as a man, and begin to carry yourself like a man who knows his value, women will pick up on this natural vibe and your dating prospects will improve dramatically.

Here are a few Game concepts to get you started.

Frame/DHV (Demonstration of High Value)
One of the first things you need to learn is how to demonstrate high value even when the deck is stacked against you. There are many ways to view the world in which you live, and the angle you choose to take is called your "frame".

For example, let's say you and another man are both trying to attract the attention of a particular young lady. During the course of the conversation, he begins showing off his new, very expensive watch.

His frame is:
"I have high value because I can afford to purchase expensive things."

Now, you yourself have a cheap watch, and everyone can clearly see that. You have two options here: you can accept his frame that he has higher value because of his fancy watch – or you can substitute your own frame by saying something like,

"Dude, $500 for a watch? You got ripped off big time! Check this out, $19.99 at Walmart in any color you want."

Your frame is:
"A real high-value man doesn't need a fancy prop to prove his value, people know high value when they see it."

Neither frame is any more or less objectively true than the other; they are merely different ways of looking at the same set of facts. So, by setting your own frame instead of passively accepting someone else's, you can essentially create a parallel reality that favors you.

For a great example of maintaining frame I will direct your attention, once again, to the movie *Titanic*.

Jack, a Third Class passenger is having dinner with a group of First Class passengers. Ruth is trying to make him feel inferior because he doesn't come from a wealthy family. Watch how he rejects her frame and substitutes his own:

> **Ruth:** *And where exactly do you live, Mr. Dawson?*
>
> **Jack:** *Well, right now my address is the RMS Titanic. After that I'm on God's good humor.*

> **Ruth:** And how is it you have means to travel?
>
> **Jack:** I work my way from place to place; you know, tramp steamers and such. But I won my ticket on Titanic here at a lucky hand of poker. A very lucky hand.
>
> **Ruth:** And you find that kind of rootless existence appealing, do you?
>
> **Jack:** Why yes, ma'am, I do. I mean – I've got everything I need right here with me. I've got the air in my lungs and a few blank sheets of paper. I love waking up in the morning and not knowing what's going to happen or who I'm going to meet. Where I'm going to wind up. Just the other night I was sleeping under a bridge and now here I am on the grandest ship in the world having champagne with you fine people.

As a man, you should always strive to set your own frame in life; and in your frame, things are always going your way.

Mistakes are learning experiences. Having your job outsourced is an opportunity to try something new. A broken leg gives you a chance to catch up on your reading. No matter what happens, your world should have a positive spin which always leads to your glass being half full.

Oneitis

Oneitis is a term that refers to getting overly attached to one particular woman prior to marriage. This pitfall stems from a cultural imperative to find "The One". As a general rule you should not be looking for one special person that God put out there just for you because, usually, that's not the way it works.

The idea of "The One" is a fairy tale straight out of Hollywood, but many people within the church have fallen for it hook, line and sinker. In his book *Love, Sex and Lasting Relationships*, Chip Ingram describes the Hollywood formula for finding love:

1. Find the Right Person
2. Fall in Love
3. Fix Your Hopes and Dreams on This Person for Your Future Fulfillment
4. If Failure Occurs, Repeat Steps 1, 2 and 3

You see, here is the premise behind the Hollywood formula: The key to finding love is finding the right person. If your current relationship isn't working, if for some reason this person doesn't fulfill all your dreams and desires, if you're not exhilarated, then you must have the wrong person.

As Chip explains later, this is what the real formula should look like:

1. Be the Right Person
2. Walk in Love
3. Fix Your Hopes and Dreams on Christ for Your Future Fulfillment
4. If Failure Occurs, Repeat Steps 1, 2 and 3[1]

You see, it's not about *finding* the right person; it's about *being* the right person. Work on being the good, Godly man that you ought to be. Hone your alpha/beta traits and become comfortable with your own masculine nature. Prepare yourself for the journey ahead of you.

When it comes to relationships, you should keep your options open, dating several women casually (but chastely!) until you find a good prospect for First Officer. There are many women out there who would make a great wife for you, so don't feel like you have to commit to the first one you feel drawn to. There is no "One" you have to find, so take your time and be selective.

The most common form of dating today is called "serial monogamy", which Wiktionary defines as:

The practice of having a succession of (especially short)

monogamous relationships with different people.

This mating strategy has become so ubiquitous that most people don't even realize that it is only one strategy among many. But, despite its prevalence, this mating strategy is actually a very poor one. Serial monogamy will drag you from heartbreak to heartbreak as you commit to a series of women who, in the end, will turn out to be a poor match for you.

By the time you find a good match, you will be emotionally spent from the search and unsure if this latest relationship will really stick. And that's assuming you don't just marry a woman who isn't right for you in order to save face or avoid the pain of yet another breakup.

Take it from someone who's been there: don't use the serial monogamy strategy. Instead, be a free agent, always dating casually but never putting commitment on the table until you are fairly certain you've found a keeper.

This is actually how dating used to be done back before the sexual revolution. Young men would date many different women, sometimes simultaneously, but they all understood that there was no commitment implied. When he found a woman he thought was good marriage material he would ask her to "go steady". Only then was his affection reserved for her alone.

That's what you want to do. You don't owe commitment to anyone but your wife, so until you find a woman who is close enough to what you are looking for to justify focusing your attention on her, you should make it very clear to the women you're dating that you are not "in a relationship".

Essentially, as un-romantic as it may sound, you should approach your search for a wife like an employer who's looking to fill a position. A company may interview a hundred candidates, but the only one who gets the company's commitment is the person it hires.

Of course, and I can't stress this enough, you must do all this while holding yourself to a strict no-sex rule. You are not a player – you are a Christian man seeking a wife. Your sex belongs to your wife and her sex belongs to you. You want a chaste woman; therefore you should hold yourself to the same standard.

---

1 Chip Ingram – Love, Sex and Lasting Relationships

Chapter Twelve
The Sexual Marketplace

How do you instinctively know when you first see a woman whether or not she's out of your league? Because you can sense her Sexual Market Value:

> *Contrary to yearnings for equality, all people simply are not equivalent in the currency of mate quality. People who are themselves high in mate value succeed in attracting the most desirable partners. In the crude informal American metric, the 9s and 10s pair off with other 9s and 10s. And with decreasing value from the 8s to the 1s, people must lower their mating sights commensurately. Failure to do so produces a higher probability of rejection and psychological anguish.*[1]

Everyone, young and old alike, has a Sexual Market Value. If a given woman's SMV is too much higher than yours, then she's out of your league. If it's too much lower than yours, then you are out of hers:

SMV, however, does have some fluctuation. If an attractive

woman is in sweatpants and her hair isn't done, she might only be a 7. But in a nice dress that accents her curves, ready to go out on the town, she might well be a 9. So, SMV can be somewhat fluid from day to day, especially for women.

Men are naturally attracted to well-proportioned, fertile women with symmetrical faces. This is because a man's body agenda is subconsciously looking for good genes to have healthy babies.[2] That means a woman is at her peak SMV when she's in her 20's and in good shape. If she maintains a healthy weight and dresses to accent her femininity, however, she can maintain a fairly high SMV for much longer than that.

But for men there is a catch. Since a woman's body agenda is seeking not only good genes, but also a good provider[2], our SMV takes a hit early on while we are young and have few resources. It eventually rises the rest of the way as we come into our own as mature men who have achieved some stability and status in our personal spheres. This causes a disparity in peak SMV between men and women:

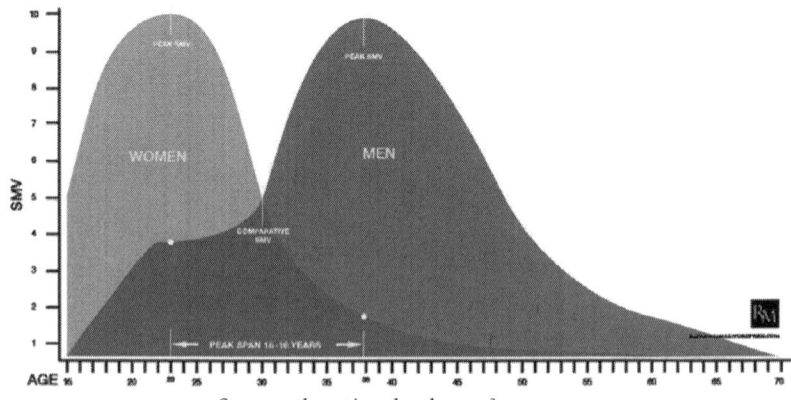

Source: *therationalmale.com*[3]

At first this may seem odd, but it actually makes perfect sense that men would reach their peak later. This disparity causes women to be most attracted to men who are a little bit older and wiser than they are – leaders ready to guide their families through the rough seas ahead.

And indeed, in most cases, we see that women naturally tend to pair bond with men who are at least a year or two older (and typically also an inch or two taller) than they are.

But, here again, our Progressive society is taking us into uncharted waters. The common refrain today is that a woman's 20's are for experimentation and fun, not to be wasted by settling down and committing to one man; and as you can see from the chart above, this period coincides precisely with a woman's peak Sexual Market Value.

Up until about age 30, women have a clear and massive advantage over the men in the dating field. But after that point the tables turn 180° almost instantaneously. Suddenly, men gain the upper hand and women find themselves scrambling to find a seat before the music stops.

In times past, the older generations would steer a young woman into marrying a man with potential. Sure, in the woman's eyes it might seem like she was settling because her value was so much higher than his, but the older generations knew that a woman's market value was fleeting while a man's market value would continue growing for years to come.

The time for a woman to land one of these up-and-comers was while her value was high and his was still comparatively low. The man benefited early on by having a beautiful, fertile bride. She benefited later by having a man who was working steadily to provide a comfortable life for herself and their children, even after her beauty had begun to fade.

What our current society is effectively doing, though, is telling women that they are entitled to spend their years of high market value having guilt-free sex with fun alpha guys. Then, they are turning around and telling the beta men that they should be sacrificing their own high market value years to create a soft landing for these women who have now (often by necessity) decided to step off of the carousel of cads and into the open arms of a waiting beta provider.

Don't fall for this trap. You don't want an "experienced" woman who suddenly appreciates your beta qualities now that her own market value is declining. These women make poor mate choices for many, many reasons.

For one thing, a large percentage of women lose their ability to properly pair-bond after only a few sexual partners. Consider this chart from *The Heritage Foundation*:

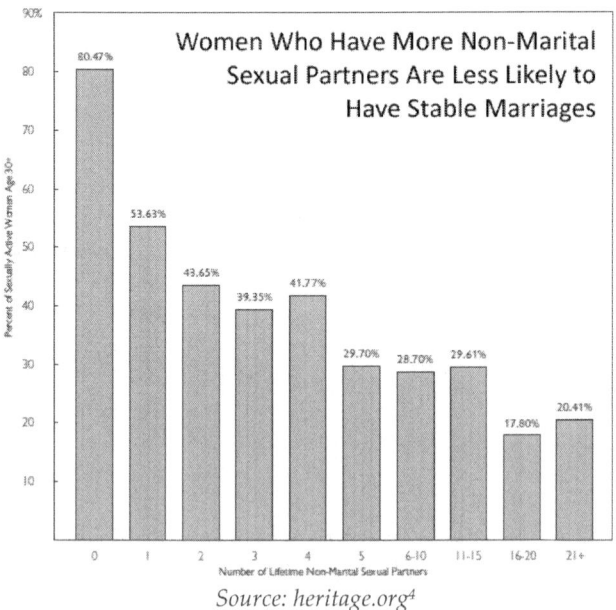

Source: heritage.org[4]

Simply having *one* sexual partner prior to marriage drops a woman's chances of having a stable marriage from 80% down to only 53%. That's a bigger difference than the drop between two partners and twenty partners. Ouch.

In addition, prior to the sexual revolution, men and women would typically pair off with someone of a similar SMV. But now that sex has been separated from marriage, women are following their natural urge to seek high value men right into the beds of men who are willing to sleep with them, but would never consider marrying them.

And because these women are bonding with men who have a higher value than they can reasonably expect to land, you can actually end up married to a woman who is objectively now a 5, but she used to be a 7 who slept with a bunch of 9's, and now looks at your higher status of 6 as "settling" – and resents *you* because she feels like she could have done better.

Keep it simple, men. When it comes to women with an extensive sexual history, just say "no".

You have a right to be picky. It's not about them – it's about you. If a woman has squandered her peak SMV having sex with a string of men, then that was her decision; it has nothing to do with you. Don't settle for scraps. This is too important. You need to find a First Officer who is worthy of the position.

Remember, it's not your job to save anybody; it's your job to find a woman who will be the best wife possible for you and the best mother possible for your children. Don't let anyone make you feel guilty for seeking a quality woman. It's your life, not theirs and the person who will have to live with your decision will be you, not them.

1 http://www.edge.org/response-detail/23862

2 http://www.independent.co.uk/life-style/love-sex/attraction/the-science-of-magnetism-926693.html

3 http://therationalmale.com/2012/06/04/final-exam-navigating-the-smp/

4 http://www.heritage.org/research/reports/2003/06/harmful-effects-of-early-sexual-activity-and-multiple-sexual-partners-among-women-a-book-of-charts

Chapter Thirteen
The Institution Formerly Known As Marriage

What exactly is in a marriage contract? Can you tell me the terms? Chances are, you only have a vague idea and not a solid definition. This is because, when you marry in a church, you are actually entering into two contradictory marriage contracts simultaneously. Confused? Don't worry, I was too. Here they are, stripped down and simplified:

Marriage Contract #1: Biblical Marriage
This is the verbal contract that couples agree to when they stand with their beloved before God and family and vow to remain together until separated by death. This contract places the couple under the authority of Scripture.

Marriage Contract #2: Legal Marriage
This is the written contract a man and woman sign in order for their marriage to be recognized by the state and/or country in which they reside. This contract places the couple under the authority of the laws of the state in which they reside.

Now, there's nothing intrinsically wrong with having both a biblical marriage and a legal marriage. The two can co-exist peacefully.

The problem is that the legal definition has changed so much in the last several decades that the two are now fundamentally incompatible; and the legal definition has superseded the biblical one to the point where married couples aren't really married in a biblical sense at all.

Oh, you think I'm exaggerating? Let's just see about that.

Marriage 1.0
Up until the mid-1900's the legal definition of marriage reflected the biblical definition pretty closely. Based on thousands of years worth of human history (not to mention a firm grasp on human nature), this contract stated that marriage was to be between one man and one woman, for life, and the union was dissolvable under only the direst of circumstances.

If one person wanted out, it was necessary to establish "fault". Whichever party was determined to be "at fault" was typically dealt with harshly during the divorce proceedings:

Common grounds for fault-based divorces include:

- *Infidelity/Adultery/Cheating*

- *Cruelty - inflicting unnecessary emotional or physical pain*

- *Abandonment or desertion*

- *Confinement in prison for defined number of years*

- *Physical inability to consummate marriage, if not disclosed before marriage*[1]

Marriage 2.0
But, beginning in the 1970s, it was no longer necessary for a

person to have a good reason to abandon their marriage vows; simple boredom was reason enough:

> *In no-fault divorces, neither party is blamed for the unravelling of the marriage. In some states a couple must live apart for a period of time, usually months, before filing for a no-fault divorce.*
>
> *All states offer the option for filing for no-fault divorce. A no-fault divorce cannot be contested or stopped by the non-filing party.*[1]

The net effect of the new legal definition of marriage was to culturally render biblical marriage null and void. Marriage vows are now mere ceremony; they are not binding at all.

The only legally binding part of the ceremony these days is the signing of the marriage license itself, and that license puts both parties under the authority of a law which says that the marriage can be dissolved by either party at any time and for any reason – regardless of what was agreed to in the vows.

In this way, marriage has become a bait-and-switch operation being carried out by the church on behalf of the state. Since the document being signed does not reflect the verbal agreement, the contract is quite literally fraudulent.

To see how this works, let's pretend a man is buying a home from a couple down the street. He verbally agrees to a sale price of $50,000 and the realtor gives him a contract to sign to make it official. Then, they all go down to the bank where the couple demands $100,000.

The man becomes very upset because he only agreed to pay half that price. But the bank examines the contract and, sure enough, the contract that he signed says $100,000. Is the contract valid?

No! This is called "Misrepresentation" and it is illegal:

> *A fraudulent misrepresentation is where someone misstates a*

> *fact and either knows or believes that what he is saying is not true or is not sure whether or not his statement is true but passes it off as true anyway.*
>
> *If a party to the contract relies on the fraudulent misrepresentation and enters into a contract based on that misrepresentation, the contract is voidable by the innocent party.*[2]

In my opinion, this is an area of willful blindness on the part of the Body of Christ. As it stands, our churches are knowingly allowing couples to enter into marriage with a fraudulent contract. Under Marriage 2.0, wedding vows no longer mean anything as far as the law is concerned, yet churches continue to perform marriages on behalf of the state anyway.

Are churches servants of the state that they should marry people with a contract that contradicts God's laws about marriage? Of course not! Marriage was God's idea, given to man long before any government was around to legislate it. Therefore, marriage supersedes any laws made by men.

Knowing this, then, how do we reclaim true biblical marriage in our churches? Honestly, I don't know. But it's high time we at least pose the question.

So, what effect has this misrepresentation had on marriage? Well, for starters, as soon as no-fault divorce was signed into law, the divorce rate in America went through the roof.

Because it's now possible for a single party to unilaterally end the marriage for any reason whatsoever, a dissenting spouse has very little recourse left to keep their marriage afloat in the face of a marital crisis.

Therefore, it is only prudent to consider the facts very seriously before you even think about tying the knot.

The Facts

Fact #1: About 50% of marriages now end in divorce.[3]
Fact #2: Women are more likely to file for divorce than men.[4]
Fact #3: During divorce women typically receive half of the marital assets regardless of the length of the marriage.[5]
Fact #4: Women get primary custody of the kids over 90% of the time, even if the marriage dissolved because she cheated on her husband.[6]
Fact #5: If she gets custody of the kids, you will be on the hook for child support at least until they turn eighteen. Sometimes you're even required to put them through college.[7]
Fact #6: Child support payments are based on your income at the time of instatement; if you lose your job or take a pay cut your child support payments often do not change to reflect your new financial situation.[8]
Fact #7: If you are unable to pay your child support for any reason, they can put you in jail.[9]
Fact #8: The court doesn't care about your visitation rights. If your ex-wife doesn't uphold her end of the agreement, nobody is likely to care.[10]
Fact #9: Some women falsely claim physical or sexual abuse in order to keep their ex-husband's involvement after divorce to a minimum.[11]
Fact #10: At least 1 out of 25 children is raised by a man who mistakenly believes that he is the father when he really isn't.[12]
Fact #11: Even if you can prove that a child isn't biologically yours, there's a good chance you will still be required to pay child support anyway in the event of divorce.[13]

Keep in mind that you could find yourself facing one or more of the above circumstances regardless of how hard you try to be a good husband and father. That's the insidiousness of no-fault divorce:

> *"A father could be sitting in his own home, not agreeing to a divorce, not unfaithful to his marriage vows, and not abusive, and the next thing he knows, the court has taken his house, his children, and a lot of his money, and then forced him to*

> *pay his wife's legal fees and even her psychologist's fees. And he can be threatened with jail time if he resists."*[14]

Now, I'm not trying to scare you away from marriage entirely, and I'm definitely not saying that all women are like this. I'm just trying to open your eyes to the simple truth that no-fault divorce is a modern reality, and it can ruin your life even if you are trying your best to do everything right.

Not only that, but divorce is marketed to women of all ages as a great way to be true to themselves and maximize their options. And if you think that this can't possibly happen if you marry a Christian woman, think again. The church's divorce rate is almost as high as the general population's, and some churches have even begun to actively encourage couples to consider divorce as an option.

This is why you need to be so, so careful when choosing a wife. You need to make this decision with both eyes wide open to the Biblical Order, the societal contract and the quality of the individual woman you are considering marrying.

1 http://blogs.findlaw.com/law_and_life/2009/08/what-is-a-fault-vs-no-fault-divorce.html

2 http://nationalparalegal.edu/public_documents/courseware_asp_files/contracts/DefensesToFormation/MisrepresentationNondisclosureDuressUndueInfluence.asp

3 http://www.divorcerate.org/

4 http://www.divorce-lawyer-source.com/faq/emotional/who-initiates-divorce-men-or-women.html

5 http://www.smh.com.au/lifestyle/celebrity/cleeses-23m-divorce-unfair--leaves-me-poorer-than-her-20090818-eo2c.html

6 http://www.law.fsu.edu/journals/lawreview/frames/254/mcnefram.html

7 http://www.divorcenet.com/states/washington/wa_art02

8 http://blogs.findlaw.com/law_and_life/2013/06/how-job-loss-can-affect-child-support.html

9 http://www.nolo.com/legal-encyclopedia/jail-time-unpaid-child-support.html

10 http://www.dadsdivorce.com/articles/how-do-states-enforce-visitation-interference.html

11 http://divorceresistance.info/dv.html

12 http://menshealth.about.com/od/lifestyle/a/paternity.htm

13 http://www.khou.com/home/Houston-man-forced-to-pay-child-support-for-child-that-DNA-proves-isnt-his-124472429.html

14 http://living.msn.com/life-inspired/sudden-divorce-syndrome-3

Chapter Fourteen
How to Find a Good Wife

Choosing whom to marry is the most important decision you will ever make, so don't go into this lightly or with your head in the clouds. God gave you a brain and He expects you to use it.

The first thing you need to know when looking for a wife is that being in love is not a good enough reason to get married. Don't get me wrong here, it is definitely necessary; but by itself it's not enough.

Forget the pop songs, forget the movies, forget culture. Your marriage is going to need more than just emotions to keep it going. How many couples are in love when they get married? How many do you think walk up to the altar thinking, "I'll bet we'll be part of that fifty percent who gets divorced"?

Trust me, love by itself isn't going to cut it.

The next thing you need to know is that you must not be unequally yoked. I'm sure if you grew up in the church you are familiar with the term, and have heard that it means that a Christian shouldn't marry a non-Christian. That's true, you shouldn't. But I'm going to take it two steps further than that.

Not only should you not marry a non-Christian, but you shouldn't even marry a Christian if her life isn't bearing the fruit that a Christian's life is supposed to show. There's a huge difference between self-identifying as a Christian and conducting one's life accordingly. You need to find a woman who lives her life according to Scripture.

Then, even after that, she needs to be a woman who understands what biblical marriage is. Feminism hasn't just affected the culture at large; it's also deeply ingrained in the church. Even if a woman doesn't consider herself to be a feminist she may still balk at the idea of submitting herself to your authority as the Captain of your marriage.

You need a woman who recognizes and aspires to the biblical model of marriage, and who will proudly tell others that she is your First Officer. If she is not seeking to submit herself to the authority of both her husband and God, then don't marry her.

Dalrock, a popular Christian relationship blogger, has a great list of questions for a young man to ask when considering a woman as his potential wife. Of course, you don't want to just show her the list, shine a spotlight in her face and demand answers. But, through the course of your conversations, you should try to discover where she stands on these issues. What you find will tell you a lot about the kind of wife she is likely to be.

> • *What does she think is the best part of marriage?*
> *Is she more interested in the wedding itself or the ring than being your wife?*
>
> • *What does marriage mean to her?*
> *She's asking you to sign on the dotted line. What's in this contract?*
>
> • *What is the role of a husband?*
> *What are the obligations of a husband? You want to be on the*

same page here, but this is also a setup for the next question. If she has a long list for you and a short one for her, that is very telling. Likewise if she rattles off the list for you but struggles to form the list for herself, you've just learned something.

• **What is the role of a wife?**
What are the obligations of a wife? The specifics are important here, but her overall attitude toward having obligations is critical as well. Does the idea of having a role to conform to or duties make her bristle? This is also your best opportunity to frame the roles the way you would expect them to be.

• **What if you are "in the mood" and she isn't (aka "wifely duty")?**
I hesitated to include this, but I feel it really should be there. Part of what this will show is her general willingness to consider your needs over her own feelings (altruism) and her tendency to look for opportunities for compromise. This will also give you a hint about her perception of male sexuality. You also want to smoke out a potential to use denial of sex for power purposes. Lastly, for men sex in marriage really is love. How would you feel about a man who decided not to hug or kiss his wife, or refused to tell her he loved her?

• **What does she think about the double standard regarding promiscuity?**
Frame this with sympathy to the feminist perspective. This is a bit of a trick question. The right answer is disgust with promiscuity across the board. The wrong answer is an instinct to shelter sluts from judgment for their actions. This question has the bonus of drawing out a feminist vibe she might be concealing, although in the scheme of things a little feminism in a young woman isn't the end of the world. But you should know what you are getting into.

• **Why does she think so many women have to date "bad boys" before they learn to look for good guys?**

Again, a bit of a trick question and should be framed non-judgmentally. Ideally she should have disgust with those girls who chased alphas while she looked for something different. A convincing story about why she made this transition isn't what you want to hear from a potential wife, but you should frame this question in such a way so this seems like a perfectly acceptable answer.

- ***What are acceptable reasons for divorce?***
This should be a short list of no nonsense answers. I'm thinking infidelity, real and persistent abuse, persistent gambling and/or addiction, etc. Scary answers include the standard "just not happy", "falling out of love", "growing apart", etc. These mean she will dump you the second things get tough or something or someone more interesting comes along.

- ***Will she judge other women who divorce frivolously?***
Unfortunately it should be easy to come up with an example of this, so mention it in conversation and see what her reaction is. How would she feel about attending the second (or third) wedding of this woman?[1]

Additionally, you want to make sure that your future wife will put your family before her career. It's more likely than not that your wife will have to work in order for your family to survive in today's world. However, you and the kids should not be accessories to her glamorous working-girl lifestyle; rather, you should be her purpose in life.

And finally, marry someone beautiful. As much as our culture likes to insist that real beauty is on the inside (and this is true in a way), you still want to marry a woman you are attracted to. There is no shame in insisting that the woman you marry be someone you find beautiful. Waking up every morning next to a woman who is lovely both inside and out will go a long way toward making your home a place you long to be.

If you put all these things together, you should have a very good chance at having a happy and healthy marriage that will be the envy of most people you come into contact with, even in these uncertain times.

---

1 http://dalrock.wordpress.com/2010/07/10/interviewing-a-prospective-wife-part-ii/

Chapter Fifteen
Conclusion

So, you now have a basic understanding of the Biblical Order, the societal contract and modern marriage. You've also seen how they impact the world around us. The question is – why haven't you heard most of this before?

How could it be that young men and women, raised in the church, know almost nothing about these important topics when they've spent their entire lives listening to sermons about how to become men and women of God? How did we manage to miss the boat so badly?

I believe the answer is twofold: ignorance and fear.

As I stated earlier, good men want nothing more than to do right by women. We don't want to be oppressive, so when the feminists began their campaign, men of the Church bent over backward to be accommodating.

But, in our effort to please women, we have abandoned the Word of God for doctrines of men. Our wilful ignorance of God's design for men and women has been disastrous for both the church and the world around us.

The second part of the equation is fear. I can assure you that I am not the only man in the church who realizes that our egalitarian society and the Word of God are completely at odds with one another. Trouble is, nobody wants to come right out and say it.

To say publicly that God has established a hierarchy and that men and women of the church ought to be following it, even in the 21st Century, is to paint a gigantic target on one's back.

Nevertheless, this is the truth. And as Christian men, it is our duty to proclaim the truth. Yes, it may make us unpopular. Yes, it will cause division. Yes, there will be a cost. What of it? Did you really think being a Christian was going to be easy? Come on, you know better than that:

> *Do not suppose that I have come to bring peace to the earth. I did not come to bring peace, but a sword.*
> *- Matthew 10:34 (NIV)*
>
> *If the world hates you, keep in mind that it hated me first.*
> *- John 15:18 (NIV)*
>
> *Then Jesus said to his disciples, "Whoever wants to be my disciple must deny themselves and take up their cross and follow me.*
> *- Matthew 16:24 (NIV)*

We are supposed to be the salt of the earth. Salt irritates a wound, but it also heals it. The message in this book may be a bitter pill to swallow, but the medicine it contains is desperately needed. It starts with you. Will you stand up for the Word of God? Will you refuse to bend a knee to the golden image of Progressivism?

I leave you with the following words:

> *"We all want progress, but if you're on the wrong road, progress means doing an about-turn and walking back to the*

right road; in that case, the man who turns back soonest is the most progressive."
- C.S. Lewis

"My conscience is captive to the Word of God. To go against conscience is neither right nor safe. I cannot, and I will not, recant. Here I stand; I can do no other. God help me."
- Martin Luther

Resources

Books

How to Answer "Do These Pants Make My Ass Look Fat" And Get Laid Like Tile
Athol Kay

Men On Strike
Dr. Helen Smith

The Married Man Sex Life Primer
Athol Kay

The Way of Men
Jack Donovan

No More Christian Nice Guy
Paul Coughlin

Love, Sex and Lasting Relationships
Chip Ingram

Websites

Married Man Sex Life
http://marriedmansexlife.com

Dalrock
http://dalrock.wordpress.com

Patriactionary
http://patriactionary.wordpress.com

The Elusive Wapiti
http://elusivewapiti.blogspot.com

Vox Popoli
http://voxday.blogspot.com

Feminism is Empathological
http://empathological.wordpress.com

Rational Male
http://therationalmale.com

Oz Conservative
http://ozconservative.blogspot.com

Things That We Have Heard and Known
http://canecaldo.wordpress.com

The Orthosphere
http://orthosphere.org

Alpha Game
http://alphagameplan.blogspot.com

Haley's Halo
http://haleyshalo.wordpress.com

Sunshine Mary
http://sunshinemaryandthedragon.wordpress.com

Unmasking Feminism
http://unmaskingfeminism.wordpress.com

Donal Graeme
http://donalgraeme.wordpress.com

The Society of Phineas
http://societyofphineas.wordpress.com

Dr. Helen
http://pjmedia.com/drhelen

Gucci Little Piggy
http://glpiggy.net

The Badger Hut
http://badgerhut.wordpress.com

Free Northerner
http://freenortherner.wordpress.com

No Ma'am
http://no-maam.blogspot.com

Delusion Damage
http://delusiondamage.com

Made in the USA
San Bernardino, CA
03 October 2013